# MAKE & STYLE
# HEADBANDS

BY THE EDITORS OF KLUTZ

**KLUTZ**®

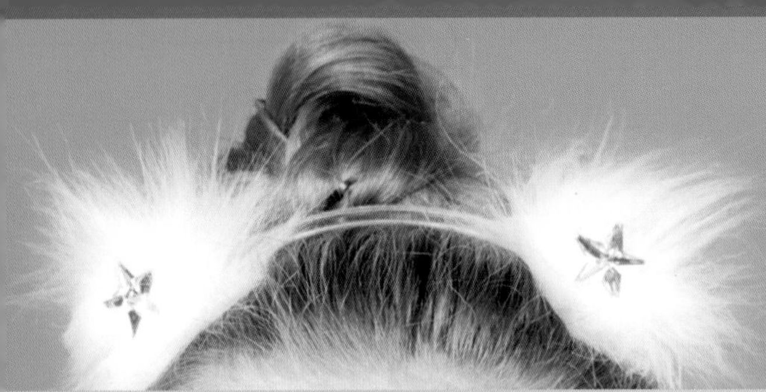



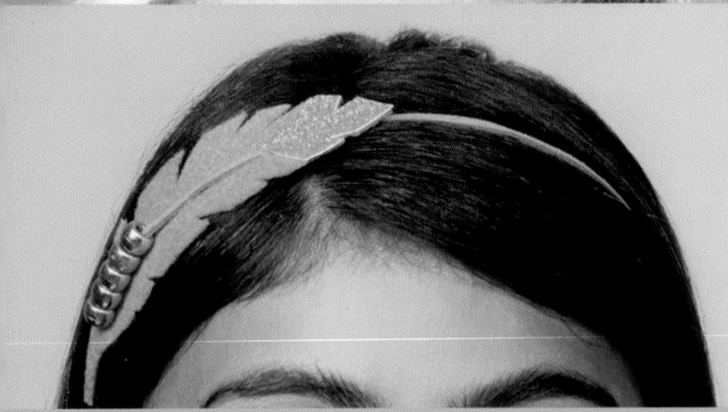



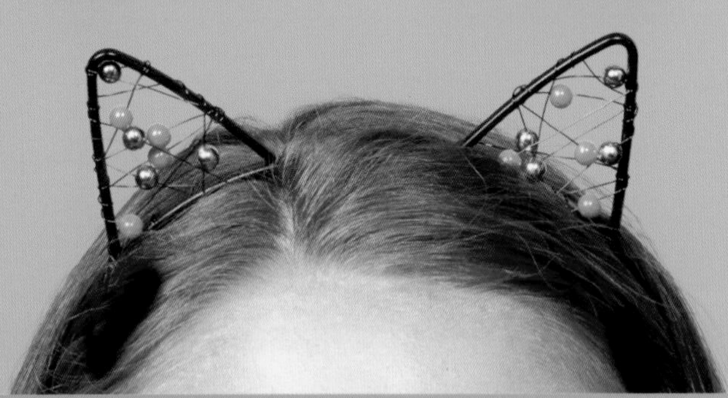



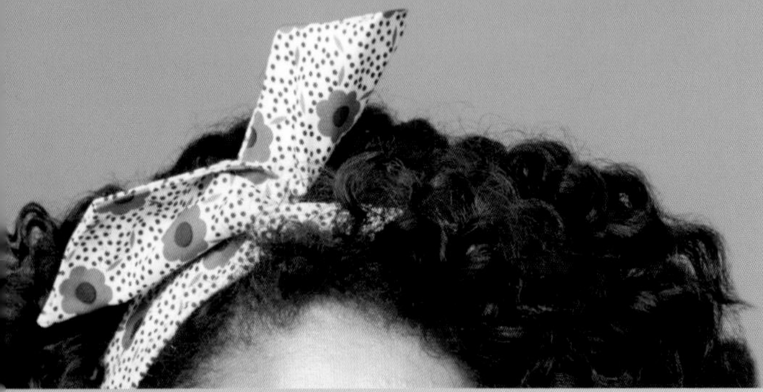



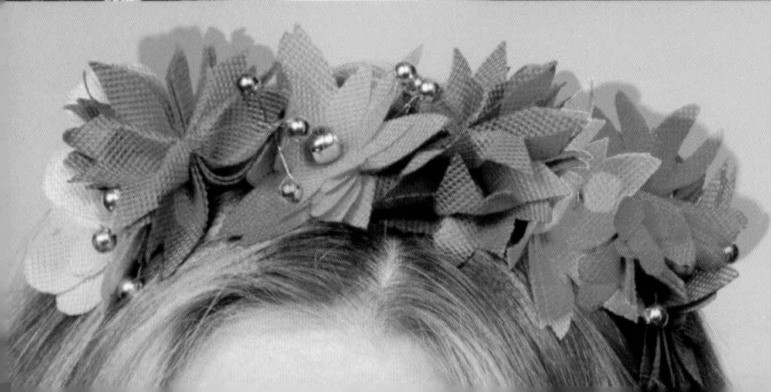

# WHAT YOU GET

**GLITTER STICKER SHEET**

**PAPER PATTERNS**

feather

flower 1 small

small star

**2 THIN WIRES IN 2 COLORS**

**FAUX LEATHER CORD**

**FABRIC IN 3 COLORS**

**THICK WIRE**

**FABRIC TAPE**

**36 BEADS IN 2 COLORS**

**FELT**

**PRINTED FABRIC**

**10 PONY BEADS**

**2 RHINESTONES**

**2 FUZZY STEMS**

**CAT EAR HEADBAND**

**2 GLITTER HEADBANDS**

# WILD CHILD

# TWIST IT!

## Learn this twisted technique to make cute and clever furry ears!

**1**  Bend a fuzzy stem in half to find the center.

**2**  Starting from the backside of the star rhinestone, lace one of the wire pieces across the front and back through the other hole.

Pull the wire until the ends are equal lengths.

**3**  Flip the star over and twist the wires together a couple of times. Leave the wire ends long.

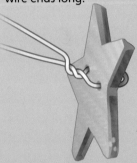

**4**  Hold the wired rhinestone against the center of the fuzzy stem with the wire tails hanging down.

**5** Wrap the wire tails around the fuzzy stem (under the star rhinestone) until you run out of wire.

### TIP:
If the fur is getting in your way, straighten the fuzzy stem until the wire is completely wrapped. Then bend it back in half.

**6**  Set aside and repeat Steps 1–6 with the other side.

# Band Together

**1** Place the wired fuzzy stem on top of the headband with the rhinestone star pointing up.

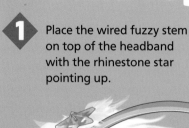

**2** Wrap the FRONT fuzzy stem back behind the headband.

This bend will force the star to fall to the side of the headband.

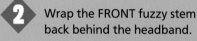

**3** Next wrap the BACK fuzzy stem foward in front of the headband.

This bend may hide the star. It's OK—it will shine again shortly.

**4** Gently adjust the star so it's in the middle of the ear and not hidden by fur.

**5** Repeat Steps 1–4 to make the other ear.

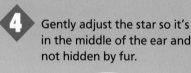

### TIP:
Use a comb to gently fluff the fur stuck in between the bends.

# BONUS BANDS

For a different look, push both ears to one side for a fuzzy fashion statement...

## Want to make more?

Now that you know how to make the Wild Child, here's your craft store shopping list:

- Fuzzy stems (most likely located by large pipe cleaners)
- Sew-on rhinestones (buttons work, too!)
- Thin wire

## ...or swap the jeweled accents for large gold beads.

**1** String three large gold beads onto the thin wire.

**2** Twist the wires together a couple of times. Leave the wire ends long.

**3** Wrap the wired beads onto the fuzzy stem (see page 5, Steps 4–5). Then attach the ears to the headband (see page 6, Steps 1–5).

# POM-POM CROWN

Dig through your craft supplies at home to give an old headband a new look.

**WHAT YOU NEED**
- Yarn
  (one pom-pom =
  12-inch (30 cm) strand
  & 4 yards (3.7 m) strand
- Dinner fork
- Headband
- Scissors

## MAKE A POM-POM

 For each pom-pom, cut a strand of yarn 12 inches (30 cm) long. Then cut a strand 4 yards (3.7 m) long.

 Lay the short strand of yarn (12 inches / 30 cm) in the middle of the fork.

3 Wrap the long strand of yarn (4 yards/3.7 m) in even wraps aound the fork.

 Pull up the short, center strand and tie it around the yarn bundle.

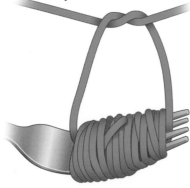

 Then slowly pull off the yarn bundle from the fork. Work slowly so the center strand doesn't come untied.

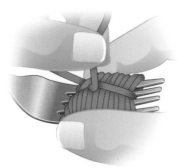

 Pull the center strand tighter and tie another tight knot.

**7** Insert scissors into the bundle and cut along the edge.

**8** Trim the pom-pom until it looks more round.

**TIP:**
If it doesn't look fluffy and round, it's probably because your center strand isn't tight enough. To fix, simply wrap another strand of yarn around the bundle and pull it tighter.

DON'T CUT THE LONG TAILS.

# PUT IT TOGETHER

**9** Tie the long tails to a headband with a double knot.

**10** Trim the long tails short so they disappear into the pom-pom.

**11** Repeat Steps 1–10 until you like the way your crown looks.

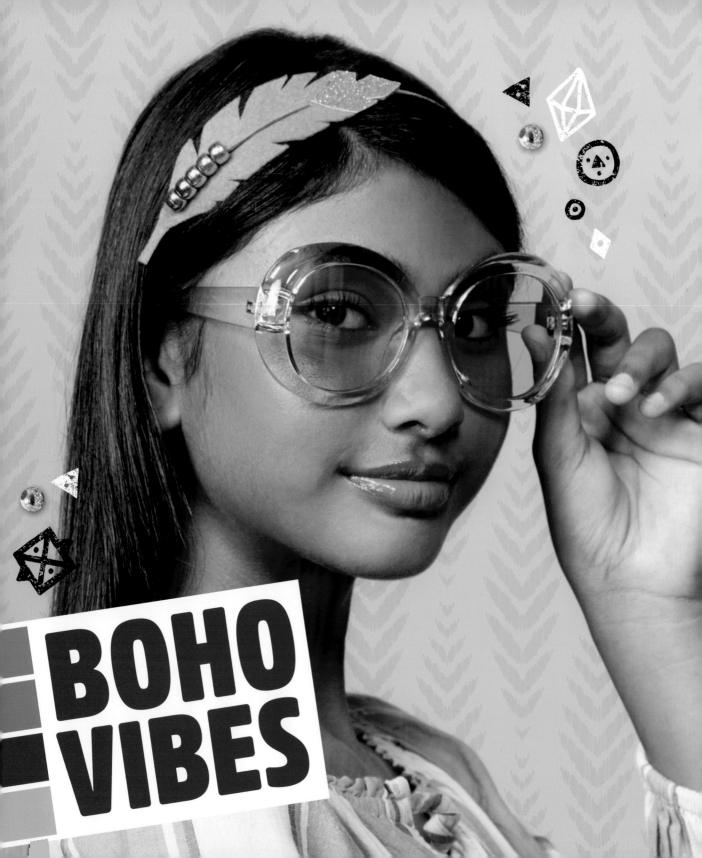

# TRACE IT!

**Trace, cut, and decorate to make this beautiful boho look.**

 Place the feather pattern on the blue felt near the edge. Use a pen to trace around the feather pattern.

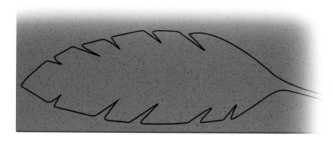

This is what the feather and feather tip patterns look like.

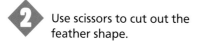 Use scissors to cut out the feather shape.

Trace around the feather tip pattern on the backside of the gold sticker paper near the edge. Cut out the shape.

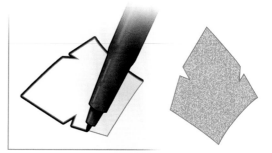

# Band Together

 Fold the felt feather shape in half. Snip two small cuts into the folded edge. Each cut should be about 1½ inches (4 cm) from the end of the shape.

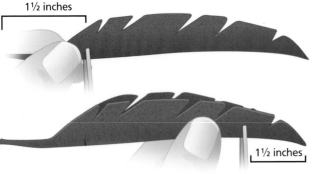

1½ inches

1½ inches

 Lay the feather shape down with the clean side up. Remove the sticker backer from the feather tip shape. Attach it to the tip of the felt feather, aligning it with the shape underneath.

 Poke one end of the cord up through the hole near the base of the feather.

 String 5 gold beads onto the cord and poke the cord back down through the second hole near the tip of the feather. Slide the completed feather to the middle of the cord.

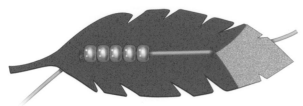

# BONUS BAND ARROWS

If feathers aren't your style, then let us point you in another direction. Use the same materials in this kit to make another look.

 **1** Trace and cut 5 triangles out of felt and 2 arrow shapes out of the glitter sticker paper.

 **2** Fold each of the felt triangle shapes in half. With sharp scissors, make two very small cuts about ¼ inch (6 mm) apart from each another in the center of the triangle shape.

 **3** Peel the sticker backer off the glittery shapes and stick them to two of the blue triangles as shown.

**4** String the triangle shapes onto the cord in the order shown, tucking each one slightly under the triangle to the left. Add beads to the plain triangles as shown in the tip below.

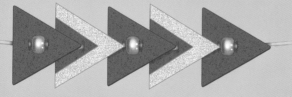

When you poke the cord up through the first hole in the plain triangles, string a bead onto the cord before you poke it back down the second hole.

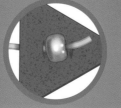

# BONUS BAND
# STARS

## Want to change directions again? Then look to the sky.

**1** Trace and cut 2 small stars and 1 large star out of felt. Trace and cut two small stars out of gold sticker paper.

**2** Fold the felt star shapes in half so that two of the points match up. Then make two very small cuts on the center of the folded edge. Make the cuts ½ inch (1.3 cm) apart on the big star and ¼ inch (6 mm) apart on the smaller stars.

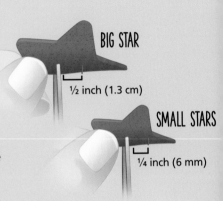

BIG STAR
½ inch (1.3 cm)

SMALL STARS
¼ inch (6 mm)

**3** String the stars onto the cord so the larger star is centered between the two smaller blue stars. When you are stringing the larger star onto the cord, add two large gold beads before you poke the cord back down through the second hole.

**4** Slide the three felt stars to the center of the cord. Then take the sticker backing off of the two smaller glitter stars and stick them onto the two small felt stars, matching the two shapes.

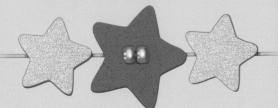

## Want to make more?

Now that you know how to make the Boho Vibe, here's your craft store shopping list:

- Felt or vinyl (any material that won't fray)
- Beads with large holes
- Cording or skinny ribbon

# STRETCHY BAND

Dig through your craft supplies (and hair drawer) at home to make new bands using this technique.

**1** Use the tip below to estimate and cut your cord/string to the correct length. Then decorate the headband with supplies from your craft drawer at home. Tie one end of the cord/string to one side of the hair elastic using a double knot.

**2** Tie the loose end of the cord to the other side of the hair band at the estimated length. Trim off the extra tails of string.

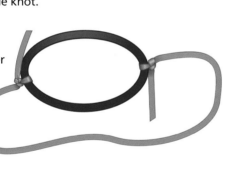

## WHAT YOU NEED
- Cord
- Elastic pony tail holder
- Scissors

## MEASURING TIPS:

Use an extra piece of string or cord to measure how long you should make your headband. Measure from the nape of the neck, up over your head where the headband will be, and complete the loop back at the nape. Add 2 inches (5 cm) to your measurement. This will be your headband length.

ROCKER
CHIC

# WRAP IT!

Learn to wrap with wire and beads and you will have a headband that is ready to rock out!

## WHAT YOU NEED

- Cat ear headband
- Thin wire, cut into two 24-inch (61 cm) strands
- 8 pink beads
- 8 gold beads

**1** Hold the end of the wire against the headband.

**2** Wrap the long end of the wire around the headband.

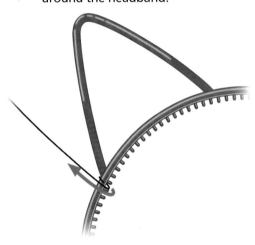

**3** Wrap the wire around the headband again to secure.

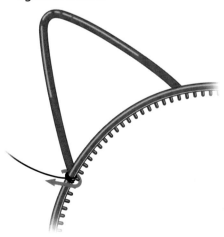

**4** Bring the wire across the ear shape until it reaches the other side.

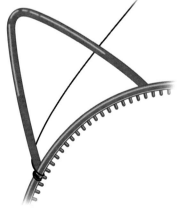

Bend the wire around the outside of the ear shape...

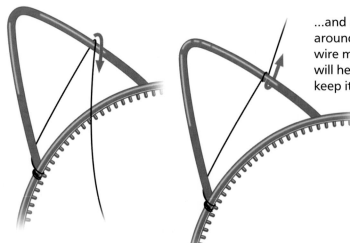

...and continue wrapping it around the ear shape until the wire makes a full rotation. This will help secure the wire and keep it from sliding around.

 This time string a bead onto the wire before you wrap it across the ear shape to the other side. Remember to wrap the wire a full rotation around the edge of the ear to secure the wire.

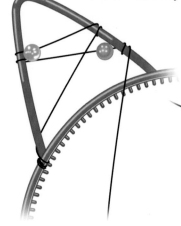

7 Continue to zigzag the wire across the ear shape, adding beads where you choose and remembering to make a complete wrap around the edge of the ear before you cross back across.

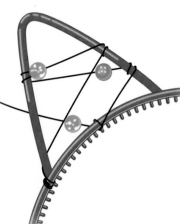

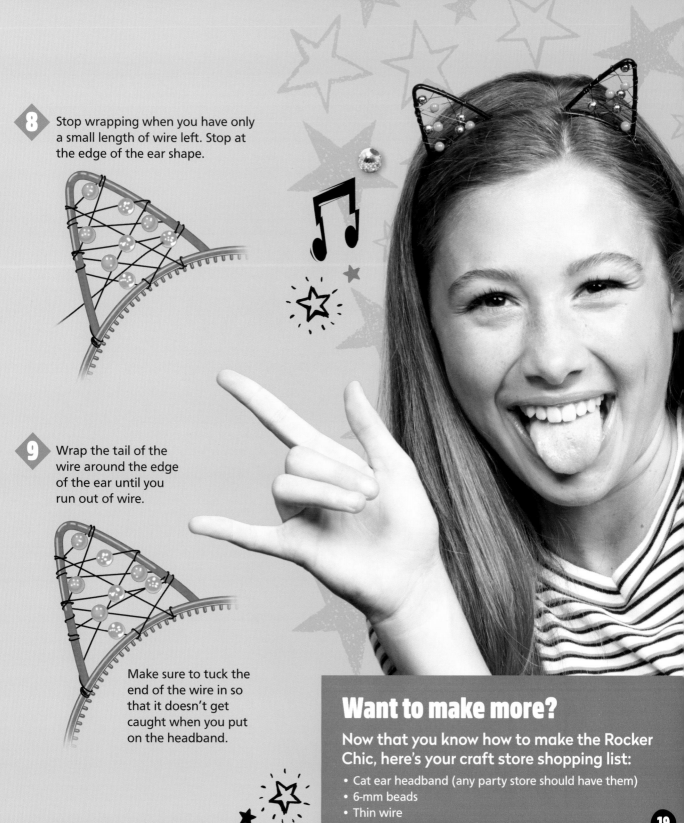

**8** Stop wrapping when you have only a small length of wire left. Stop at the edge of the ear shape.

**9** Wrap the tail of the wire around the edge of the ear until you run out of wire.

Make sure to tuck the end of the wire in so that it doesn't get caught when you put on the headband.

## Want to make more?

Now that you know how to make the Rocker Chic, here's your craft store shopping list:

- Cat ear headband (any party store should have them)
- 6-mm beads
- Thin wire

# RIBBON EARS

Dig through your craft supplies at home to make a new set of ears.

**1** Trim both pipe cleaners to 8 inches (20 cm). Start with one pipe cleaner.

**2** Bend the pipe cleaner in half to make a point (like the tip of a cat ear).

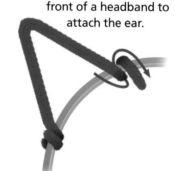
**3** Wrap the ends of the pipe cleaners onto the front of a headband to attach the ear.

**4** Repeat Steps 1–3 on the other side.

Step back and make sure they are the same size. Adjust if needed.

### WHAT YOU NEED

- Satin ribbon (2 yards/1.8 m)
- 2 pipe cleaners
- Skinny headband
- Double-sided tape or fabric tape
- Gift wrap tape or masking tape

**TIP:**
Wrap some tape around the ends to make sure the ears stay in place.

## WRAP IT UP

**1** Put a piece of double-sided tape close to the bottom of the end of the headband.

**2** Place the end of the ribbon going longways against the headband.

**3** Wrap the ribbon around the end to cover the tape.

**4** Continue to wrap the headband in even rows.

**5** Wrap over the pipe cleaner ends and right up and around the first ear.

**6** Once the pipe cleaner is covered, go back to the left to wrap the exposed headband.

**7** Keep wrapping up and around the ear a second time.

**8** Contine to wrap and follow Steps 5–7 on the second ear.

**9** Once you reach the opposite end of the headband, add a piece of double-sided tape on top of the ribbon.

**10** Tack the end of the ribbon down and trim any extra ribbon close to the headband.

You can make other ears, like bears or bunnies. Just adjust the shape.

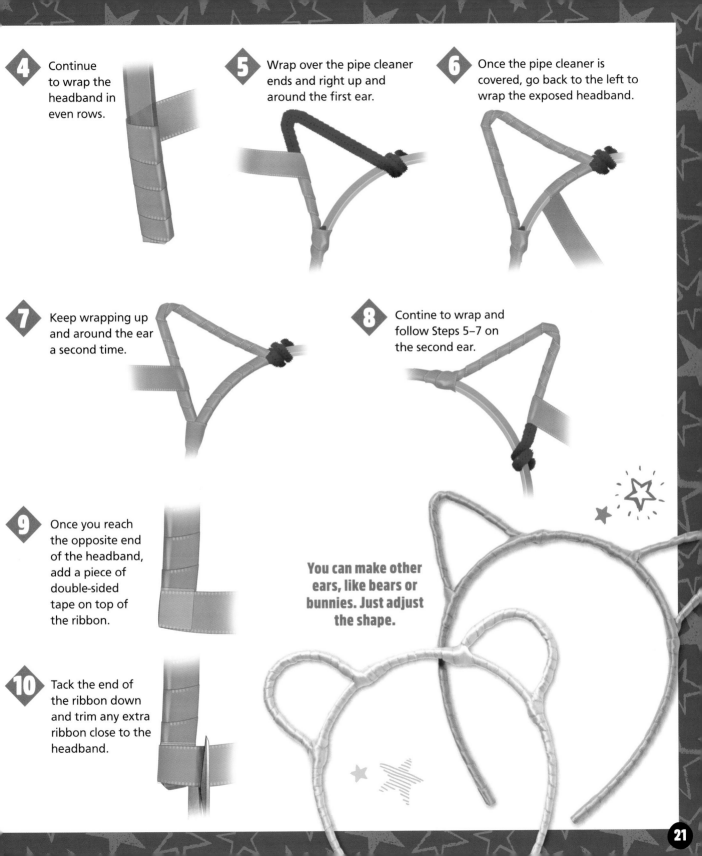

**LEADING LADY**

# FABRIC BAND

**A totally trendy take on retro style.**

 Start with the wrong side of the fabric facing up.

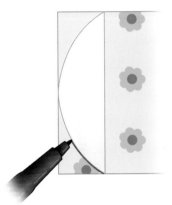

Line up the curve of the pattern on the short edge of the fabric. Then trace the pattern with pen or chalk.

 Trim along your traced edge. Repeat on both ends of the fabric.

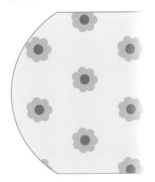

**TIP:** Eventually you will fold the end to a point. This step will help make a perfect point.

 Stick a piece of fabric tape along the entire bottom edge of the fabric (lengthwise).

 Smooth down the entire piece of tape to make sure it's really stuck down.

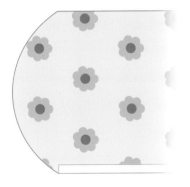

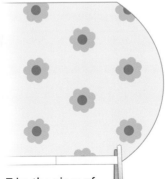

Trim the piece of tape once you reach the other end of the fabric.

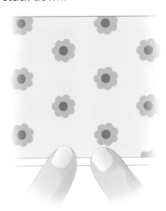

**5** Gently remove the paper backer to expose the sticky side of the tape.

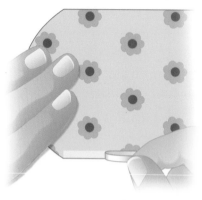

**6** Begin to fold up the edge of the fabric the width of the sticky part of the tape. Continue to work slowly to fold up the entire bottom edge of the fabric.

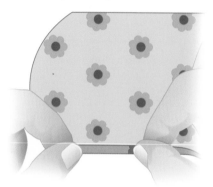

**7** Smooth down the entire fold to make sure it's really stuck down.

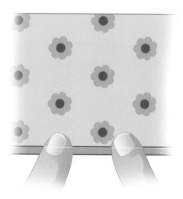

**8** Repeat Steps 3–7 on the other side.

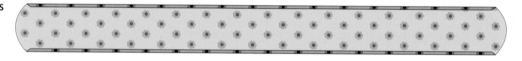

**9** Stick a piece of tape at an angle to the middle of the curved edge.

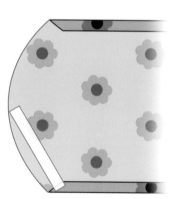

Remove the paper backer and fold the fabric over the exposed sticky part of the tape.

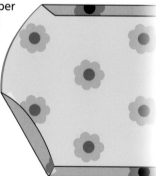

**10** Add another piece of tape on top of the folded point down on an angle to the other side.

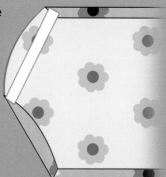

The end should look like this:

 **11** Repeat Steps 9–10 on the other end of the fabric.

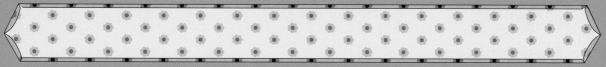

# The Wired Band

 **1** Bend the end of the wire about 2½ inches (6.4 cm) down to make a hook.

**2** Twist the end of the wire around itself to make a secured loop.

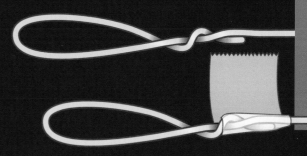

**TIP:**
Wrap a piece of tape (from home) around the end of the wire so the wire will be soft against your head.

 **3** Repeat Steps 1–2 on the other end of the wire.

Finished, the total length of the wired band should be about 30 inches (76.2 cm) from left to right.

# Band Together

 **1** Stick a short piece of fabric tape ONLY on the left side of the top folded edge of the fabric. Smooth it down, then remove the paper backer.

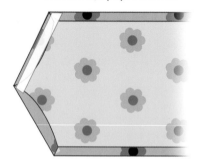

 **2** Next stick a piece of fabric tape along the entire top folded edge of the fabric (lengthwise). Smooth down, then remove the paper backer.

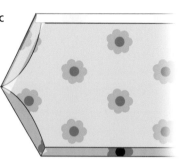

It should look like this:

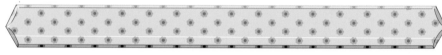

**NO TAPE ON THE RIGHT EDGE, YET!**

 **3** Fold the fabric down in half so the edges line up. Press firmly along the edges to make sure the tape sticks.

You should have a long pocket with the right side of the pocket still open.

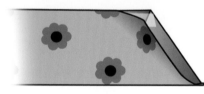

 **4** Slightly fold back the open end (the right side) of the pocket and gently slide the wired band into it.

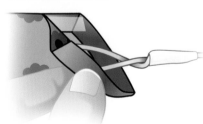

 **5** Once all the wire is covered, stick another piece of fabric tape onto the folded edge. Smooth it down, then remove the paper backer.

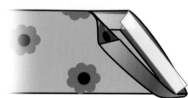

 **6** Close up the end and press the edge together to make sure the tape sticks.

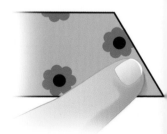

# HOW TO
# STYLE

**1** It's super simple. Slide the headband under your hair and criss-cross the ends at the top of your head.

**2** Twist the ends around each other one or two times, depending how long you want the ends to look.

# BONUS BAND
# TWIST KNOT

**For a different look, just tie the band in a different way.**

**1** Slide the headband under your hair and crisscross the ends at the top of your head.

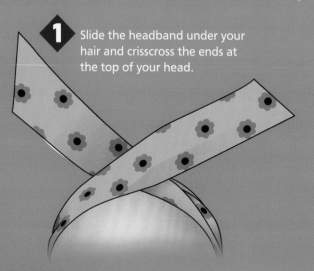

**2** Twist the ends around each other once and lay both sides down so that they're flat against your head.

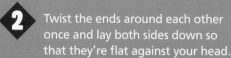

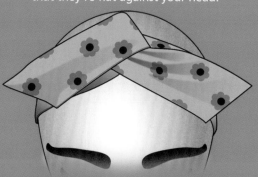

**3** Tuck the ends under to create a knot.

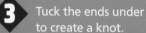

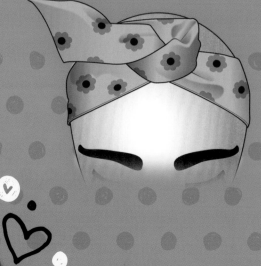

# WIRED PONY BAND

**Dig through your craft supplies at home to make a new band.**

A pony band is just a shorter version of the headwrap. Cut a strip of fabric that is 14 x 3 inches (35.5 x 7.6 cm) to make your pony band. The wire should be 17 inches (43.1 cm) long.

## WHAT YOU NEED

- Fabric
- Double-sided tape or fabric tape
- Pipe cleaner or thick wire

# FLOWER GODDESS

# BLOOM IT!

**Give your hair some awesome blossoms!**

## TRACING AND SPACING TIPS:

To get the most use out of the fabric included in this book, you can use the page layout diagrams below to plan and trace your flowers.

# STACKED FLOWERS

**1** Use a pen to trace around the large flower pattern.

**2** Use scissors to cut out all five of the flower shapes.

Trace two more large flower shapes. Then, using the smaller flower pattern, trace two more smaller flower shapes.

**3** Starting with the large petal shapes, stack the petals on top of one another, staggering each petal layer. The two small petals should be on top.

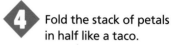 **4** Fold the stack of petals in half like a taco.

 **5** With sharp scissors, make two very small cuts about ¼ inch (6 mm) apart from each another in the center of the folded petal stack.

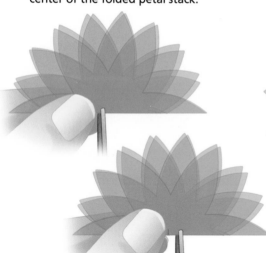

 **6** Unfold the stack of petals. Poke the wire from the bottom up through one of the slits in the layered stack of petals.

Then loop the wire back down through the second hole in the flower shapes.

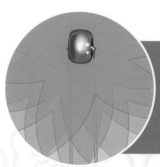

**TIP:**
For extra bling, string a bead onto the wire before you loop it back down through the second hole.

**7** Adjust the wire so that the two ends are about the same length below the petals.

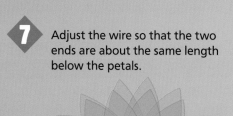

**8** Take the two wire ends and twist them together beneath the petals a few times.

To learn how to attach your flowers to a headband, turn to page 37.

# FOLDED FLOWER

## WHAT YOU NEED

- Fabric
- Edge stencil
- 6 inch (15.2 cm) piece of thin wire

**1** Cut three pieces of material, each 2½ inches wide and 3 inches long (6.4 cm x 7.6 cm). Neatly stack the sheets on top of one another. Use the edge stencil to trace along both vertical edges of the stack. Use scissors to cut each side of the stack.

**2** Fold them up about ½ inch (1.3 cm) from the bottom.

½ inch

**3** Continue to accordian-fold the stack of sheets.

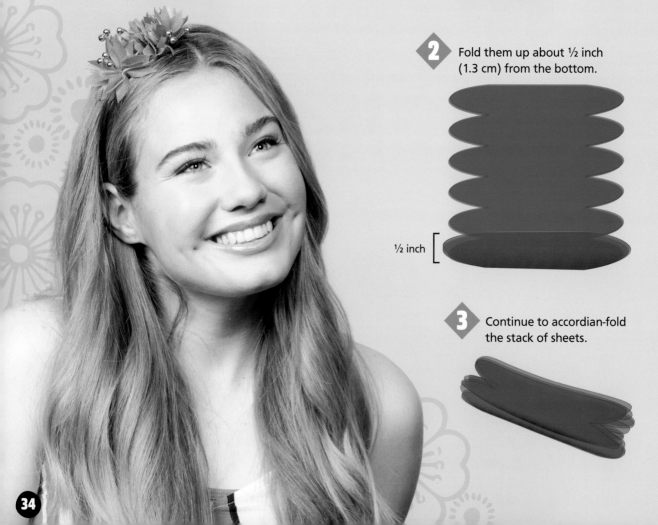

**4** Pinch the stack.

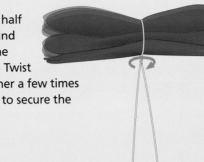

**5** Fold the wire in half and slide it around the middle of the accordian stack. Twist the wires together a few times under the stack to secure the layers together.

**6** Find the outside edge of the top layer of material on one half of the accordian stack. Gently pull that layer away from the rest of the paper. Follow that same layer all the way to the opposite end, carefully separating it from the stack as you go.

TAKE YOUR TIME TO AVOID RIPS.

**7** When you get to the end of the first layer, find the edge of the next layer and separate it in the same way. Continue separating one layer at a time until one side of the stack is completely fluffed.

**8** Repeat Steps 6–8 on the other side of the stack.

To learn how to attach your flowers to a headband, turn to page 37.

# BRANCHES

## WHAT YOU NEED

- 3 small gold beads
- 12-inch (30.5 cm) piece of thin wire

**1** Bend the wire over about 4 inches from one end of the wire. Slide a bead onto the wire so it sits at the bend.

**2** Hold the two wire ends together below the bead. Use the other hand to pinch the bead and begin to twist it around in a circle.

Continue to twist until you have about 1 inch (2.5 cm) of twisted wire.

1 inch

**3** Pull the longer wire end up and then bend it back down about an inch away from the twisted part. Slide a bead onto the wire so it sits at the bend.

**4** Again, hold the two wire ends together while you twist the bead around in a circle until the twisted wire section reaches the bottom of the previous wire twist.

**5** Follow Steps 3–4 to twist a third bead branch.

**6** Hold the two wire ends together below where the three twisted sections meet. With the other hand, grab the three twisted branches together and twist in a circle until you have about ½ inch (1.3 cm) of twisted wire below where the three branches join.

# BAND TOGETHER

## Attach your flowers and branches to the headband.

 **1** Hold the finished flower against the flat outside edge of the headband with the wire tails hanging down.

 **2** Wrap the wire tails around the headband until you run out of wire. Slide the flower to the position you want it on the headband.

Add as many or as few flowers and branches to your headband to create a look that is uniquely you.

## Want to make more?

Now that you know how to make the Goddess, here's your craft store shopping list:

- Plastic party tablecloth or tulle
- Wide-hole beads (pony beads)
- Thin wire

## BONUS BAND
# PRETTY KITTY

**Add a few flowers to the cat ear headband for a new look.**

# RIBBON FLOWER

Dig through your craft supplies at home to make a new band.

**1** Locate the wire in the ribbon. Pull out about 3 inches (7.6 cm) from one side.

## WHAT YOU NEED
- Wired ribbon (any width) 36 inches (91.4 cm) in length
- A shank button

**2** Slide a button onto the exposed wire. Tie a knot near the ribbon end to secure the button, leaving a wire tail.

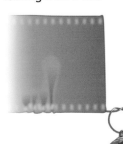

**3** Locate the wire on the opposite end of the ribbon. Make sure it's the same side the button is attached to. While holding that wire, push the ribbon down toward the button.

**Turn the page to finish up your ribbon flower.**

 **4** The ribbon will ruffle and make a spiral-looking shape.

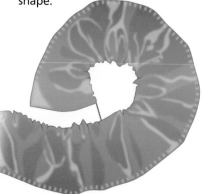

 **5** Go with the natural curve of the ribbon and curl the ribbon into a circle shape.

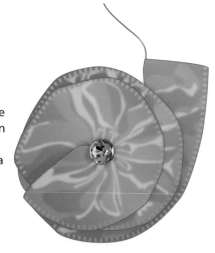

 **6** Flip the flower over. Find the shorter wire tail coming from the button end and twist it together with the longer tail to secure the shape. Cut the longer tail to match the length of the shorter tail.

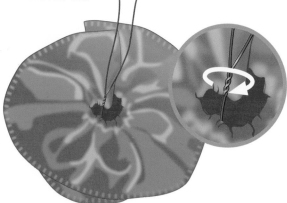

**7** Attach the ribbon flower to the headband (see page 37).